My Little Book of Divinity - Verses to Empower & Awaken Your Spirit!

Shweta Velkar

Presentation by *BookLeaf Publishing*

Web: www.bookleafpub.com

E-mail: info@bookleafpub.com

ISBN: 9789358731361

First edition 2023

DEDICATION

I dedicate this book to everyone who is trying their best to make it in life.

To all my fellow humans - This book is as much yours as it is mine. I am only writing it on behalf of us all!

ACKNOWLEDGEMENT

I would like to thank God Almighty, for infusing this wisdom into me and giving me the strength and ability to share it with others!

I would also like to thank BookLeaf Publishing for organising this challenge, which gave me the opportunity to share these divine poems with everyone in the form of this "Little book of Divinity."

LOVE

"Let me introduce myself - I AM LOVE..
Not the kind you humans share,
But the kind that is showered from up above.

I know not expectations,
Nor any terms and conditions,
All I know is an unconditional acceptance of
divinity's myriad creations.

I do not share space with fear, worry, anger, or
hate,
When you choose me, these emotions will be
shown the exit gate.

I follow a simple rule - I ALWAYS start with the
SELF,
And to truly experience me,
guilt and judgement you must shelve.

So today I come forth, with this simple message
for you -
Let go of everything that is not me, for..
You are me,
And that, my friend, is the only TRUTH."

- AARYA (Shweta Velkar)

FRIENDSHIP

Friends are family outside of home,
They treat you like a treasure, and not like a
possession they own!

A true friend stands by you through thick and
thin,
And without judging you, he guides you to look
within.

He helps you to recognise your worth,
And when you're feeling "not good enough,"
His motivation knows no dearth!

A friend can play the role of a teacher, parent,
and guide,
Who will accompany you on life's
roller-coasters and never leave your side.

A friend knows when you're sad,
And he also knows when you've been bad,
But through it all,
Just to have you in his life, he will be glad!

If you do not currently have such a friend, then
be one to someone,
And if you are fortunate to have such a gem,
then revere them like they are 'THE ONE!'

Treat them like a treasure, and do not let this
saga end,
Because believe me dear one,
TRUE FRIENDS are indeed your best blend!

- AARYA (Shweta Velkar)

A CHAT WITH GOD…

"Dear God, Oh Creator, Our Source,
I wonder why I feel so much force –
Force to do things just to comply,
And I thought that I was an individual in my
own right!"
To which God replied –
"Your only obligation was to yourself,
You chose to feel the pressure, we never said.
That happened because..
You had to learn - how to be YOU without any
dread.
Not for a minute did I leave you alone,
All your experiences only served to remind you
that….
You are……. MY CLONE."

- AARYA (Shweta Velkar)

EMOTIONAL WORKOUT

The current state of the human race,
Is more fear and less the "ability to face."
Add to this, the EGO, which in its entire grace,
Has fully nourished emotions that
lie at the base of the vibrational space.
Anger, Jealousy, Greed, Envy and Guilt
Have now over spilt.
Propelling digression from the core and fuelling
Self-Doubt,
Don't you think it's time for an upgrade by
getting ourselves an
EMOTIONAL WORKOUT?

\- AARYA (Shweta Velkar)

DO YOU TOLERATE?

Mark the date..
When you Tolerate.
As you fail to see..
That in doing so, YOU AGREE!
Do you realize that before injustice when you
bend,
Your consent you thereby lend?
Which makes them believe they have the right to
abuse,
And they happily make YOU their muse!
And then when this you realize..
You feel victimized.
So stand up for yourself,
It's about time your boundaries you clearly
demarcate..
So that …
There is never a DATE on which you have to
TOLERATE!

- AARYA (Shweta Velkar)

WHY SHOULD I...

Why should I…
Try to look good to the eye..
That judges me on the sly.
Why should I?

Why should I...
Try to impress those..
Who constantly live a lie...
Why should I?

Why should I…
Try to appeal to those who imply
That it's not enough just being 'I'
And so, I must try...
Why should I?

Why should I..
Try to smile when I want to cry..
Only to join them in their lie?
Why should I?

I say enough is enough..
Now the only reason I will try...
Is so that upon myself I can rely...
Others can continue to deny...

I am done living this lie...

And I still continue to think...

Why Should I???

- AARYA (Shweta Velkar)

ASSERTIVE YOU…

I am afraid to speak my truth -
For fear of being judged and ridiculed..
So, I sadly repress what I believe,
For years on end, until I see..
This is not what was expected of me!
All I had to learn to do, was lovingly express
myself fearlessly.
And now..
An assertive heart and a courageous path were
calling out to me,
And asking me to be brave enough to be
authentically me.
This wasn't always easy, but with faith and
divine decree,
I now walk a path of
ASSERTIVE AUTHENTICITY!

- AARYA (Shweta Velkar)

FREEDOM

The illusion of the Earth plane, doesn't let you
see,
That as a powerful being of light, you are always
free!
The mind likes to make you believe - that you
are trapped, helpless and meek.
As that is how it is able to keep you discreet!

Feelings of Entrapment and Enslavement,
Are just but the mind's boo-boos,
For as spirit incarnate, you are completely free –
And that, right there my friend, is the divine
truth!

- AARYA (Shweta Velkar)

EMPOWERMENT

Look in the mirror, and tell me what you see.
Is it a powerful soul or is it all the fallacy?

Do you see being the result of all of life's battles
won?
Or do you see the failures and setbacks wishing
there were none?

Do you see a spirit with a spark in the eyes?
Or do you consider yourself unwise?

Now let me tell you the truth of who you are –
You are a fragment of the divine, no matter the
scars!

You embody wisdom, beyond your might,
You hold within you, God's divine light!

You are always in charge of your life,
Because don't forget, you have the power of
choice!

You can always exercise this power,
And create what you desire.

So, if you ever feel down and out,
Look into the mirror and know this without a
doubt -

You are more powerful than you give yourself
credit for,
Your life is proof of how much you can endure!

So, rightfully own your power and live your
truth,
As that is true EMPOWERMENT embedded at
the roots!

- AARYA (Shweta Velkar)

GUARDIAN ANGELS

I know I have angels watching over me,
They know me inside out, even better than me!

I call out to them when in doubt,
And with their unending grace they always reach
out.

They give me so many signs letting me know,
That no matter what I'm going through, I'm
never alone.

With them by my side, I know I can face,
Whatever lies ahead, with courage and grace.

And so today, I say this with great humility,
"Dear Guardian Angels thank you for always
loving me!"

- AARYA (Shweta Velkar)

ONENESS

The human species is funny in many ways..
It differentiates one from the other on the basis
of race.
This calls for a definite upgrade – A realization
that…
Colour, caste, creed, gender is all just the
surface.
What truly matters is..
To remember that we are all facets of the same
divine grace..
Just like parts of the same body, but each, with a
different face.
When this awareness takes over the human race,
We will fully experience love and kindness,
And this then, would truly reflect ONENESS!

- AARYA (Shweta Velkar)

A CONVERSATION WITH LIFE

Me: Why Oh Life, must you be so hard?
Why at times do I feel so charred?

Life: Lo and behold this truth dear one,
I am merely offering you experiences for battles
to be won!

Me: But how can I win battles, when I feel so
crushed?
Sometimes low, sometimes dusted, and
sometimes even death-brushed!

Life: No lovely one, let me make you aware,
I am not the only one responsible for all your
dares.
You made a plan, before you came to earth,
To learn all you could, to remember your worth.

Me: How can I ever be so stupid as to plan,
Something so harsh and something so bland?

Life: These plans are made with love, with no
intent of hurt or pain,

The only objective of your experiences is that of
maximum soul gain.

Me: How can my soul gain through so much
pain?
What was I thinking, was I vain?

Life: No dear one, you are a brave soul - full of
courage and strength,
You took on these lessons and experiences
because you believed in yourself!

Me: My faith and belief are shaking, and I am
breaking.
I think I need help, as I cannot keep faking..

Life: You have all the help available, if only you
remember to ask,
Your guardian angels and divine guides will ease
your tasks.
They stand tall, surrounding you at all times,
They protect and guide you, making sure you're
fine.

Me: How do I invoke their grace? And will they
make life easier to face?

Life: All you have to do is ask, and they swoop
right in,

Once you feel their presence, you can always
win.
Things do not feel as intimidating and
overwhelming with them by your side,
Now you can simply focus on learning your life
lessons, so that your soul can smile.

Me: What if I still fail, what if I still fall?

Life: Failure is a perception, NO ONE fails at
life's call!
Learn to believe in yourself and in your divine
team,
You are the master of your life, and capable of
achieving your dreams!

Me: Thank you life, for reminding me of my
strengths!
Is there any other wisdom that you would like to
lend?

Life: Happy to help!
And please remember that I am your friend.
When things get rough, rely on your strengths.
Now before we end this chat,
Let me give you a life hack –
Everything that you experience,
is for your highest good,

Remember this always, and you will then have
understood -
The true meaning of life in all its chaos galore,
That it is not just God, but you who are a
powerful co-creator!
You dear one, are powerful beyond means,
You just need to remember that I unfold the way
that you choose to perceive!
So, own this power, and create me like art,
And let's be the best of friends, till death do us
apart!

- AARYA (Shweta Velkar)

FAITH – THE MIRACLE WORKER

"I am Faith.
I decide your fate.

They call me the miracle worker,
As I am indeed your safe harbor.

You cannot hold me in parts - You either have
me fully or you don't,
You cannot say – "At times I have faith, but
sometimes I don't."

I most certainly cannot co-exist with fear and
doubt,
That is something I must live without.

There is a reason they say that I can move
mountains,
I resonate with the frequency of the Divine
fountain!

When you go through life's phases and cycles,
You need me the most, to work you miracles.

Despite what life may be throwing at you,
If you choose me, I promise I'll see you
through!"

- AARYA (Shweta Velkar)

COMPASSION

When I hurt you, or you hurt me,
It is very easy to get angry.
But this time I suggest,
That we both pause and take a rest..
Let us remember that we are both appearing for
life's various tests,
And sometimes dealing with these can be a
mess!
So, the next time I hurt you or you hurt me,
We shall both pause and see..
See that we each have a story – A story of a
unique journey,
And we will just let each other be.
For, as fellow living beings, the least that we can
do,
Is understand that not all that we perceive may
be true.
We can choose to remember, that we are all part
of the same source,
And that something may lie buried within the
other's closed doors!
Something that may be painful or hurtful or even
nasty,
Thus, making it important to let the heart see –

That not everything is about you, but about
another's history!
And when this kind of perception becomes a
tradition,
It is then that we, as a race, will have truly
mastered Compassion.

- AARYA (Shweta Velkar)

KINDNESS

Whenever you get the opportunity – Be Kind!

The human heart,
Is a divine part.

Nothing is yours or mine,
In the end it is all about being kind!

Kind to each other, kind to ourselves,
Kind to all those who need our help!

When given a chance, grab it with both hands,
Just be kind and don't expect a thanks!

Be kind because that is who you are,
Be kind because everyone's fighting an inner
war.

Be kind because that is what is rare,
Be kind because what is needed the most right
now is care!

Be kind because nobody would dare,
To invest time on another, to stop and stare.

You be the one who changes this for the world,
Because kindness is something that will create a
swirl.

Be kind when it is least expected,
Set an example until this gets wholly accepted.

Be a trendsetter,
Induce everyone to think – "What does it take to
be kind?"
And let them realise that it's simpler than a
blink!

Be the way shower,
Be kind to one and all,
Show them how it's done,
And let the darkness fall!

Make kindness a way of life, and spread this
message of love,
And this is how you'll truly represent the
divinity of source, our creator up above!

- AARYA (Shweta Velkar)

GRATITUDE

If you must wear an 'Attitude,'
It may as well be one of 'Gratitude.'

For a grateful heart, has mastered the art,
Of living with strength and contentment as a
divine mark!

If you stay deeply entrenched in gratitude,
Abundance will love your vibrational altitude.
It will rush to you without delay,
For, with a grateful heart, it must stay!

Even joy and happiness cannot evade you,
With gratitude in your heart, they must invade
you!

Love, money, peace as well,
In a thankful heart, happily dwell!

Gratitude is not just about giving thanks,
But about feeling truly blessed - for having been
gifted all the supportive hands!

It is about knowing the worth of all that you
have,
And firmly believing that you are truly God's
'chosen one,' and an integral piece of his divine
plan.

So always stay thankful and humbled with
grace,
And know that someone up there truly loves
you,
To have shown you life's beautiful face!

- AARYA (Shweta Velkar)

THE DISCERNING SOUL

This world is full of variations,
All of God's unique creations.
While some I like, and some I don't,
There is a crucial skill that I need to hone -
I need to learn how to step back,
And observe in a manner that is detached.
Viewing everyone for who they are,
Instead of, for what they lack.
Becoming aware that –
While some may align with me, and some may
not,
This in no way establishes right or wrong!
All I need to do is embrace this diversity exactly
as it is,
And remember that each of God's fragments is a
necessity and priceless.
This ability to see and accept everything as
divine and whole,
Is the true mark of a DISCERNING SOUL!

- AARYA (Shweta Velkar)

INTEGRITY

In today's world when everyone lies,
To themselves, and to others far and wide,
Being honest and true,
although rare virtues,
Must relentlessly be pursued.
We must let the masks fall off, and embrace our
truth,
It is okay to be flawed, that's the human root.
Beneath multiple layers, we hide our light,
And spend eons to find ourselves, with all our
might.
We mistake the journey, for a constant fight,
Not realising, that this is not a strife.
All that is needed, is to want to be ourselves,
And once this desire arises,
The universe will light the way.
The entire process is nothing but an unpeeling -
Of all the layers under which various parts of
you have been reeling.
All they want is your love and acceptance,
To feel safe to show themselves, after years of
suppressed existence!
Now is the time to be your own friend,
And let all your woes end.

Journey within and find your light,
Then rise back up with all your might!
But this time round you are empowered and
aware,
Because now you know your truth, and honesty
is your flair!
Fearlessly doing that which feels right,
Following your heart and your divine light.
Freely expressing and living your Authenticity,
Seeing your soul finally smile, as you now live
in TOTAL INTEGRITY!

- AARYA (Shweta Velkar)

SHIFTS..

I am slowly reaching a state where -
I want to 'Speak' less, and 'Listen' more..
I want to 'Analyse' less, and 'Understand'
more..
I want to 'Argue' less, and 'Discuss' more..
I want to 'Know' less, and 'Learn' more..
I want to 'Think' less, and 'Feel' more..
I want to 'Suppress' less, and 'Express' more..
I want to 'Please' less, and 'Help' more..
I want to 'Rescue' less, and 'Empower' more..
I want to 'Stress' less, and 'Smile' more..
I want to 'Hold On' less, and 'Let Go Of' more..
I want to 'Control' less, and 'Surrender' more..
I want to 'Resist' less, and 'Accept' more..
I want to 'Struggle' less, and 'Breathe' more..
I want to 'Try' less, and 'Just Be' more..
I want to 'Fear' less, and just 'LIVE'
.............more.

- AARYA (Shweta Velkar)

AN HONEST PRAYER

Dear God,
Please accept my honest prayer.
Can we somehow reverse the order of the cares?
Can we make PEACE a norm, and WORRY
rare?
Can we label MONEY as just a resource, and
not some scare?
Can we make ONENESS a social compulsion,
and DISCRIMINATION a dare?
Can we make KINDNESS a highly necessary
trait, and term ABUSE as unfair?
Can JUDGEMENT be discarded, and
DISCERNMENT be aired?
Can we normalise AGEING HEALTHILY, and
eradicate the belief that "With Age, I Must
Bear"?
Can BLAME and ANGER be treated as grave,
while ACCOUNTABILITY and OWNERSHIP
as fair?
Can we please label FREEDOM as the truth, and
ENTRAPMENT as illusion's dishonest glare?
Can we convert OWNING OUR POWER into a
valuable life hack, and BLIND COMPLIANCE
into a soul slack?

And how can I forget, the master of them all, can
FEAR please be eradicated once and for all?
This dear God, is a heartfelt prayer,
From my heart to yours, now that I am aware –
That humanity really needs a change of scene,
Because, what is considered normal today, is
actually obscene!
While those who walk the path of love..
Are scorned upon, I tell you the nerve!
Which is why dear God, before you I humbly
bow,
Please reverse the order of the world,
I guess it's time now!

- AARYA (Shweta Velkar)

DEATH OF THE EGO

"Oh, it hurts!" I cried.
"I know… it's necessary," God replied.

Me: Why this unbearable hurt and pain?

God: Trust me, it's not in vain.
For your soul to grow,
You must let go of all that is not you,
and, i.e., the EGO.

Me: I understand that,
But oh, today, it's my back!
While yesterday, it was my head that took the
flack!
And on some days, my emotions run wild,
While on others, I feel like a child.
Why must the process be so dense?
Why can't it be a smooth cleanse?

God: Understand this dear child,
You are releasing emotional piles - toxicity and
heaviness accumulated over time.
It is not the process that is painful,
But your resistance that makes it feel so,
It doesn't have to be this way,

So, for once, please just surrender and go with
the flow.

Me: Dear God, can you please help me through
this process of growth and expansion?
I sometimes forget that I am spirit in human
incarnation.
That I have it in me to endure it all,
That all this is for a higher purpose; it's for a
divine call!

God: Yes dear child, we never leave your side.
We understand it can feel intense, and can
sometimes give you a fright.
We always hold and protect you in our warm
embrace,
As you learn to transcend the ego, with dignity
and grace.
Just remember - this journey that you traverse, is
from you to YOU,
You are learning to conquer emotions that once
overpowered you!
You are breaking free from the shackles of
limiting beliefs and traits,
It is time to live your power, and remember that
you are spirit incarnate!

This process may seem painful, because you are
letting go –
And walking back to spirit, requires…
the DEATH OF THE EGO!

- AARYA (Shweta Velkar)